D1292767

Alexander Fleming and Penicillin

Sir Alexander Fleming
by T. C. Dugdale

JAMES PRENDERGAST LIBRARY
509 CHERRY STREET
JAMESTOWN, NEW YORK 14701

Pioneers of Science and Discovery

Alexander Fleming
and Penicillin

W. Howard Hughes

A design by Fleming done in
microbes—the St. Mary's
Hospital Medical School badge.

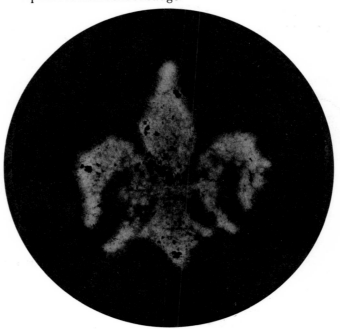

Wayland

Other Books in this Series

ISBN 85078 120 5
Copyright © 1974 by W. Howard Hughes
Second impression 1976
First published in 1974 by
Wayland Publishers, 49 Lansdowne Place, Hove, Sussex BN3 1HF
2nd impression 1979

Text set in 12/14 pt Photon Baskerville, printed by
photolithography and bound in Great Britain at
The Pitman Press, Bath

Contents

Illustrations

Introduction: Fleming the Man

This is the story of a man who did not wish to be known, who hid his views on everything except his work from all who came into contact with him. He had little use for conversation and expressed himself only through the work of his hands and his experiments. His shyness was such that throughout his career he kept a barrier around himself which was rarely crossed and only then by his more intimate friends. To his colleagues at work he would make only the most fleeting reference to his home and family life, or to his club and his hobbies. He was equally silent at his club; anyone who questioned him about his work could expect only the shortest of answers. At home in Chelsea—when he was at home, for he spent most of his evenings in the laboratory—he would entertain his friends from the Chelsea Art Club and at his house in the Suffolk countryside where he spent his weekends and holidays, he would involve himself with his family, his gardening, games and sports. So completely did he separate these sides to his life that he had three nicknames, one for each situation, and very few people knew more than one. At work he was known as Flem or, rarely, the Prof; at home he was Alec; and at the club he was Sandy.

Since no one was admitted to all three circles it is clear that any life story of him will be more than usually biassed and will only touch by hearsay on two thirds of his life. I first knew him as an inaudible and boring lecturer and later on as a critical senior member of staff. Finally, for the last sixteen years of his life, he was my direct chief. During that time we started tolerating each other and gradually, in spite of the difficulties due to our different natures, we came

first to a working partnership and finally to a friendly understanding.

The driving spring in his mechanism was the desire to find out, to establish facts, to understand, to solve a problem. After that he would lose interest. Writing and talking about it was left to others. He always needed a spokesman. Never really part of a team, he nevertheless needed someone to work near. He was a lone wolf, but once he had pulled down his quarry he would quickly grow tired of it. Much that he started was finished by other people, and if there was no one around to take it up it was dropped while he followed up new, different, more exciting ideas. He wrote well but spoke badly and was hard to hear. Little wonder he was misunderstood.

Another problem for those who tried to make him out was his sense of humour. It often went undetected, being strictly of the "deadpan" variety. Any invented or mistaken information that was printed about him he not only left uncorrected but even went out of his way to see that it was spread still further. Many of the stories that are told about him must therefore be highly suspect. I have included here only those I can confirm.

Sir Alexander Fleming as head of the Wright–Fleming Institute. He became head in 1946 when his superior, Sir Almroth Wright, retired.

1 *The Strange Route to St. Mary's*

Alexander Fleming was born in 1881 on a lonely farm called Lochfield in Ayrshire, bordering on Renfrewshire and Lanarkshire. His father, a hill farmer, had married twice, having four children by each marriage. Alec was the second youngest.

When they were not at school, Alec would explore the hills and the moorland with his brothers and sister. Hunting—without guns—and fishing developed his powers of observation. From a very early age, Alec had a love of sport which was to last throughout his life, and which was to play a big part in determining his career.

Life at the farm was secluded—their nearest neighbours were a mile away. Only at the village school at Loudoun Moor, or at the "kirk," would

Fleming revisiting the school house in Loudoun Moor, the nearest village to his childhood home, Lochfield Farm.

Alec have met anyone outside his own family, and the school had one class of only twelve or fifteen children with one school mistress.

At the age of ten, Alec moved on to the school at Darvel, the nearest town. He would make the four mile walk in all weathers. He worked well there and at the age of twelve went to the Academy at Kilmarnock for about eighteen months.

Alec's father had died when he and his brothers were still very young and they had few memories of him. His mother, Grace, was left to run the farm with the help of the eldest son, Hugh. The Flemings were not a poor family, but knowing that the farm could not support more than one of them, the rest of the family now had to earn their living away from home.

Two of Alec's older brothers, Tom and John, were already in London by the time he had finished at Kilmarnock. Originally intending to be a family doctor, Tom had soon specialized in eye diseases, becoming an "oculist," and John was learning to become an optician. Alec, now fourteen years old, travelled south to stay with them and was followed six months later by Robert, his younger brother. For the next two years he attended lectures at the Polytechnic School in Regent Street and, at the end of it, found himself a job, as a clerk in a shipping office. He did not enjoy the work in the least but he had little choice. He needed the money.

In 1900, when the Boer War became serious, John, Alec, and later Robert joined the Territorial Army. They enlisted in the London Scottish, a regiment largely composed of men of Scottish descent. Most of the men never saw any action. The number of volunteers was far greater than the needs of the British Army at that time. However, the London Scottish gave Alec a superb opportunity to indulge in his love for sports. In fact, all three brothers played in the water polo team, and Alec turned out to be quite a good shot too. To everyone's surprise, "H" Com-

THE London Scottish Regimental Gazette

No. 150.—Vol. XIII.]   JUNE, 1908.   (Price 4d. Annual Subscription, 3s.) Post free.) [Entered at Stationers Hall

"DAILY TELEGRAPH" CUP TEAM.

PHOTO KEENES & CO.]   MARCHING TO VICTORY.   [WOKING.

Above The Clarence Memorial Wing of St. Mary's Hospital, Paddington. The laboratory in which Fleming discovered penicillin was at the right front corner of the building, third floor up.

Fleming stayed in the London Scottish for fourteen years and was a distinguished member of their shooting team for most of that time. *Left* The front page of the June 1908 issue of the *London Scottish Regimental Gazette* showing Fleming (front row, left) as part of the team that carried off the *Daily Telegraph* cup at Bisley.

pany—traditionally the most awkward bunch in the regiment—carried off the shooting trophy, largely due to Alexander Fleming.

He would, perhaps, have remained in the business world all his life, but his Uncle John, a bachelor, had died in 1901 leaving him just enough money to take up his brother John's suggestion that he should go to college to study medicine. He entered for a University of London Scholarship in Natural Sciences and won. In fact, he passed top of all United Kingdom candidates, in July, 1901.

He intended to be a surgeon, perhaps specializing in eye diseases like his brother, and chose to go to St. Mary's Hospital, Paddington, out of a choice of twelve possible London medical schools. He made this choice for no other reason than that he had played water polo against them for the London Scottish, and had liked them. This, as will be seen, turned out to be a very lucky decision.

Because of the time he had spent as a clerk, he was a little older than most of the others in the class, but he never regretted the fact. "I gained much general knowledge," he said, "and when I went to medical school I had a great advantage over my fellow students, who were straight from school and never got away from their books into the school of life." He was a brilliant student, taking most of the prizes and qualifying in the shortest time. When he took his final University of London Examinations he got honours in five subjects and the University Gold Medal. Still intending to be a surgeon, he also took the Fellowship examination of the Royal College of Surgeons.

His outstanding success in examinations might give the impression that he worked very hard and all the time but this was not so. He had a very good memory and he found the work interesting and easy. He managed to find plenty of time for his sports—shooting and swimming.

For the second time now, sport was to play a vital role in determining the course which Fleming's career was to take. There was a young doctor in the bacteriology department called John Freeman who was on the lookout for people to strengthen the St. Mary's shooting team at Bisley. He knew that Fleming was a good shot and badly wanted him to stay at the hospital. Unfortunately, there was only one surgical vacancy at St. Mary's and it was far from certain that Fleming was going to get it. After a good deal of persuasion, Freeman managed to win Fleming over to the idea that he should work in the bacteriology department. All that Freeman now had to do was to convince his "chief," Sir Almroth Wright, to make the invitation.

It was not a difficult job. Freeman did not try to hide his reasons for wanting Fleming. He pointed out quite bluntly that Fleming was good with his hands, worked well and had a scientific mind, but most important of all, he was a good shot and would be just the man for his precious shooting team. Wright was amused and so Fleming was welcomed aboard.

Almroth Edward Wright (1861–1947), head of the Inoculation Department, St. Mary's Hospital. This photograph was taken in France during the First World War, and shows him in the uniform of a full colonel.

14

It was a strange place for young Fleming to find himself. He was the complete opposite to everyone there. He was state educated, a scholarship boy from a polytechnic. He was small, shy, very quiet and reserved and spoke with a broad Scottish accent. He found himself surrounded by ex-army men, mostly officers and mainly from the older universities and public schools. They were tall men—several more than six feet tall. They called Wright, who was the most senior officer among them, "the Old Man," just as a ship's crew call their captain. Fleming had one thing in common with all these others. He adored the Old Man and wanted only to please him.

Fleming was one of the second generation of bacteriologists in Britain. Whereas the pioneers of a science have to find their way entirely alone, those who follow on are taught at least some of the subject. The directions for further investigation are often set by the teacher, at least to start with, and Fleming and the other students who were attracted to Wright were put to work on the things that interested him. We can now try to see what life was like for them.

Nowadays research work is paid for by grants and studentships, and laboratories are part of a university or of the Health Service. At the end of the Boer War the position was quite different. Research was done as a hobby, paid for out of other earnings or private funds.

Wright, like a number of more senior workers in the department, had a private practice. Private patients were persuaded to give money so that research could continue at the voluntary hospitals. The young men in the laboratories would devote their evenings to such research—after a full day's work in the hospital.

At four o'clock there was tea in the library, a very small room at the top of a turret staircase. It was originally meant to be a nursing sister's sitting room. A small table, a few kitchen chairs and a couch was all

A lecture given by Dr. Cheatle of St. Mary's some time during the first decade of this century. Fleming is fourth from the right in the front row. First on the right is Bernard Spilsbury.

that there was in the way of furniture. A kettle on a gas ring provided boiling water and tea was served in an odd collection of cups and mugs. There was enough food to keep them going until ten o'clock when there was a second tea before they went home. Some would stay on even later if the work was interesting or had to be finished that night.

The main purpose of the four o'clock meetings was to talk about work. They were, in effect, lessons, tutorials, "teach-ins." The results of the previous day's experiments would be reported and they would all discuss them. After this Wright would talk about any new ideas he had had and, finally, they would plan the night's work.

The late night meetings were similar but they were often attended by visitors who would come there to talk with Wright. These included his old friend George Bernard Shaw, the playwright, statesmen like Lord Balfour and industrialists like Arthur Guinness.

Fleming came to these meetings and learned from them, but they were not the sort of occasion that really suited him. He was for the most part silent and made no conversation. If he had to report he did so in the shortest possible way. His value was at the bench not in the library.

Because of this way of organizing things it was almost impossible to tell who was responsible for the ideas that emerged. In this type of "round the table" discussion, the idea that comes out at the end and on which an experiment is based is so different from the first suggestion that no one can claim, or deserves, the credit.

Thus for the first part of his career Fleming was forced to work as part of a team. All his work in those days was the result of the efforts of the group as a whole. It was to be twenty years before he published anything that could be said to be entirely his own.

Far right Almroth Wright in the 1890s when he was the chief pathologist at the Army School of Medicine, Netley Hospital. *Centre top* A ward and *centre bottom* a hospital staff parade at Netley Hospital in the 1890s.

18

2 *Almroth Wright and Bacteriology*

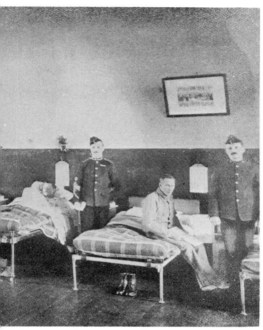

Who was Wright? He and Fleming were to work together for nearly fifty years.

Almroth Edward Wright was a parson's son. He went to school in various towns in Europe and went to college in Ireland. He had an Irish father and a Swedish mother. With this background and a passion for languages he learned to speak seven and understand five others.

In 1892 he became a professor in the army, teaching the men in the Royal Army Medical Corps and in the Indian or Colonial Medical Corps to study

Left Tents of the Royal Army Medical Corps in South Africa during the Boer War.

Left Tents of the Royal Army Medical Corps in South Africa during the Boer War.

the diseases that attacked British troops overseas, especially in hot countries. The work that they did together helped to pinpoint the causes of a great many tropical illnesses.

Typhoid fever, a frightening and often fatal disease, got special attention from Wright. In 1896 he announced that he had made a "vaccine" which would prevent it and in 1899, when the Boer War broke out, he tried to persuade the War Office to use his vaccine on the troops. The War Office was so unhelpful, and used his vaccine so badly, that in 1902 Wright left the army in disgust and went to St. Mary's Hospital as Professor of Pathology. This was about the same time that Fleming started there as a medical student.

Many of the brightest students went on to Wright's department. Some stayed for only a year or two and then went on to follow some other line of work. Others remained in the laboratories for the rest of their lives. Those lives, however, might well be short, for nothing was then known of the risks that laboratory workers ran. Two of Wright's team, Noon and Wells, were to die from diseases caught from their work. Nurses and medical students in those days were also constantly at risk, particularly from tuberculosis.

The team was originally made up of Captain Douglas (who had come out of the army with Wright), Bernard Spilsbury, John Freeman and Leonard Noon. Spilsbury soon left to start out on a famous career using science in the detection of crime.

Freeman was very good looking, tall and an athlete. He had interrupted his studies at Oxford to join the Yeomanry in the Boer War. A most charming man—his patients adored him—he was always full of ideas, but was upset whenever they were opposed. "He blew in, blew up and blew out," a colleague once said of him when he was in one of these moods. He and Leonard Noon were among the first full time allergists in the world and pioneered the successful treatment of hay-fever and many types of asthma,

Left Military stores tents used as wards for typhoid at Bloemfontein, South Africa, during the Boer War.

particularly those due to animals such as household dogs and cats, and feathers in bedding.

Fleming joined the team in 1906 shortly followed by Leonard Colebrook. Colebrook was a very different type. The son of a parson, he had intended to become a medical missionary but Wright had persuaded him to work in the laboratory instead. He was greatly devoted to his work. He later moved to Queen Charlotte's Hospital where he concentrated on deadly childbed fever. Through his efforts many lives were saved and much pain and discomfort avoided. His work in this field of medicine was as great as Joseph Lister's on antisepsis (the killing of germs) was to surgery.

Freeman, Fleming and Colebrook were each in their own way very valuable men to Wright. Freeman

Left "The Old Man"—Almroth Wright. These silhouettes were made by Handrup of D. H. Evans, Oxford Street.

Below John Freeman (1877–1962).

Left Leonard Colebrook (1883–1967) and *right* Alexander Fleming.

was his devoted admirer and a great talker—always starting off ideas. Colebrook was steady, reliable and his lifelong friend. Fleming brought skill to the invention of new methods and could carry out experiments so carefully that he outdid everyone else in accuracy. Wright called them his "sons in science," and this really does indicate the family feeling of the place at this time.

What exactly was the work that these men were doing? Very broadly speaking they, and bacteriologists throughout the world, were trying to find out how the body learns to destroy the disease organisms that invade it and how they could help the body tackle this job more effectively. Wright's experience in hot countries, particularly Egypt and India, led him to concentrate on vaccines that would prevent illness. To see how his work fits in to the way medical knowledge was developing we must go back, briefly, to the discovery of bacteria in 1683.

Antoni van Leeuwenhoek was one of the first users of the microscope. In 1683, he found that rain water, after contact with city air, contained "little animals" ten thousand times smaller than the water fleas which he could see with his naked eye. He also found and drew little animals taken in tooth scrapings from inside his own mouth. Leeuwenhoek, however, saw no connection between these "germs," or "microbes," and the causes of disease. Discovery of bacteria and other tiny animals was one thing; proving that they cause diseases was quite another.

The first man to show that one of these minute germs does cause disease was an Italian, Agostino Bassi. He spent twenty years studying the disease *muscardine* in silkworms, and showed that it is due to a tiny fungus. Thirty years later in 1866, the Frenchman Louis Pasteur, also working on diseases in silkworms, showed that the disease *pébrine* was caused by a living organism too—and one that actually lived, grew and bred inside the silkworm itself!

Above Louis Pasteur (1822–95) the French microbiologist whose work not only proved the germ theory of disease but who also pioneered immunization.

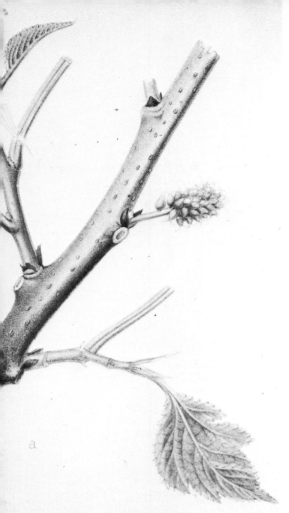

The first disease affecting man that Pasteur tackled successfully was anthrax. This disease normally attacks sheep and cattle, but sometimes it spreads to man. The anthrax microbe, called a "bacillus" because of its rod-like shape, was discovered in the blood of cattle dead from anthrax by the German Franz Aloys Pollender in 1849. In 1868 a Frenchman, Casimir Joseph Davaine, showed that these tiny bacilli were present in every case of anthrax that he came across. That, however, was not enough to prove that they caused the disease. Proof came in 1877, when Pasteur managed to produce absolutely pure cultures of these bacilli. When he injected them into test animals in the laboratory, they produced anthrax just as surely as an injection of infected blood. This proved beyond doubt that, in the case of anthrax at least, the germ theory was right. The biggest step was still to come.

A drawing from Pasteur's *Studies of Silkworm Disease*. These studies strengthened his suspicion that micro-organisms were directly related to diseases in animals and in man.

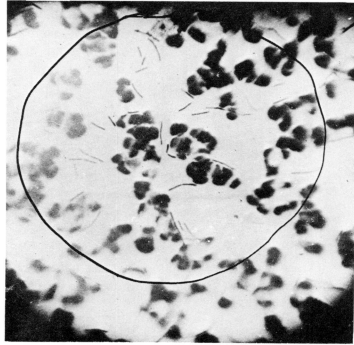

Anthrax bacilli. This photograph was taken on 20th March, 1885. The bacilli show up as short dark lines.

In 1880, Pasteur was working on the bacilli of another disease: fowl cholera. He discovered that their harmfulness could be reduced or "attenuated" by growing them in special ways. Not only that, but when he injected his chickens with an attenuated culture of fowl cholera, they became immune to the effects of future injections of the *unweakened* germs which would normally have killed them. This he then applied to anthrax. In May of 1881, in a much-publicized test, he injected twenty-five vaccinated and twenty-five unvaccinated sheep with anthrax proper. The vaccinated sheep were completely protected. Not one died. All the unvaccinated sheep were dead in less than a week. Pasteur had a similar resounding success with rabies. Pasteur's life and achievements changed the face of modern medicine. Before Pasteur most doctors refused to admit the existence of germs at all—in spite of the mounting evidence to the contrary. But, backed up by followers and pioneers such as Joseph Lister in Scotland and Robert Koch in Germany. Pasteur succeeded in breaking down the opposition to this new approach to disease. His spectacular results for immunization against anthrax and later against rabies forced even the rather conservative medical profession to accept his ideas.

Two big questions now needed answers. The first was how, exactly, does the body destroy the germs that invade it? One of Pasteur's students was a Russian, Elie Metchnikoff. Working in Italy in the early 1880s, Metchnikoff showed that the white cells of the blood pick up and digest certain invading bacteria—but did not get very far in explaining how they did it. The answer was obviously related in some way to the answer to the second question, that is how does the body *learn* to kill germs? For it was evident that the body does learn. Several people had shown that the blood after an illness would kill the germs causing that illness much more effectively than it would if it had never had the illness before. Many diseases like

Above Robert Koch (1843–1910), the German bacteriologist who built on Pasteur's work in microbiology, showing which of a wide range of bacteria caused particular diseases. He developed a way of classifying bacteria and of proving whether particular bacteria were the causes of a disease or just innocent bystanders.

Above right Joseph Lister (1827–1912) was one of Pasteur's foremost supporters in trying to get the germ theory of disease accepted. He was an English surgeon and the founder of antiseptic surgery. Shortly afterwards, Lister showed how to avoid it.

Right Elie Metchnikoff (1845–1916), the Russian biologist who showed that the white cells of the blood "eat" certain invading bacteria.

measles, mumps and chicken pox you only catch once. Furthermore, if you give a *vaccine* to a person then you may be able to teach his body to kill the germ without it having the disease at all. This was what fascinated Wright. How does the body gain immunity?

Wright also thought that it might be possible to treat disease by giving a vaccine in just the right dose to make the body do better than it was already doing. That is, vaccinate in order to *cure* as well as vaccinate in order to *prevent* disease. It was this curative aspect of vaccines on which Wright's department concentrated.

In those days there were, in theory, three approaches to the treatment of patients who already had a disease. The first was by methods of *immunology*. In

Above Young Fleming doing an "opsonic index" in the Clarence Wing Laboratories in 1909. Almroth Wright had found out that white cells would attack bacteria all the more readily in the presence of certain substances called opsonins. An opsonic index is a measure of how much opsonin is present in someone's blood. In the background, Captain Hayden, paralysed in both legs by polio, is doing routine work from a wheel chair.

these methods the body is stimulated to produce its own, natural defences against bacteria. This was the method favoured by Wright in his research. Secondly, there was the use of *antiseptics*, chemicals which kill any form of living cell. Fleming was later to show the limitations of this type of chemical. Thirdly, there were a few chemicals called *chemotherapeutic agents,* which somehow singled out certain germs, certain living cells, and killed them without greatly harming other body cells. Mercury had been known since 1493 to help to cure syphilis and quinine had been used against malaria since about 1630. But these substances were very few and far between. Wright certainly, and also Fleming to begin with, had grave doubts about the usefulness of such substances. Most bacteriologists at that time had, in any case, received very little in the way of chemical training.

There was, however, one bacteriologist who was also an outstanding chemist. He was a German called Paul Ehrlich.

There are a range of coloured chemical dyes which

Right A seventeenth century woodcut showing mercury being used as a cure for syphilis.

MERCVRE.

Private 606.
to
Sir Almroth Wright
& Co. 1930.

Ronald Gray 1911.

Above Paul Ehrlich (1854–1915), the German scientist and one of the pioneers of bacteriology. He developed the drug salversan(606) some of which he sent to Fleming to test on patients suffering from syphilis. This was one of the first modern *Chemotherapeutic agents*.

Left Private "606"—a cartoon by Ronald Gray of Fleming in 1911.

are used to stain bacteria or certain cells in body tissue. This is done to make them easier to see under a microscope. Ehrlich alone had the idea that if these dyes could be made poisonous to the bacteria which they stained then you might have something like a "magic bullet" (which kills only villains) with which to attack disease. The problem was finding a way to "load" the dye with poison and still keep it aimed at its special target. After years of work on a series of dyes called anilines, to which Ehrlich tried to attach such poisonous things as arsenic and antimony, he at last came up with a success. It was number 606 in the series and became known simply as "606". Some of it was sent to Wright. The testing of this new substance, however, was left to Fleming. After all, it was a chemical. Wright was only interested in immunity. He

thought of "606" more as a curiosity than anything else.

Ehrlich had started out in the hope of producing a drug that could be used against the venereal disease syphilis. Syphilis was greatly dreaded, quite common, and at that time incurable, although it could be controlled to some extent in some patients with mercury. Physicians, however, never had anything to do with the disease and always left its care to surgeons.

There were quite difficult surgical problems involved in giving the drug to patients. Because so little of it would dissolve in water, it had to be made up in huge volumes. It also had to be prepared in sterile conditions and given immediately by injection into a vein. Although getting blood out of a vein had been done for hundreds of years, putting anything into one with any success was a comparatively recent accomplishment. Blood transfusions and "intravenous" injections are everyday happenings now, but then they

Above Paul Ehrlich in his study at the Hoechst Dye Works. In 1908 Ehrlich shared with Metchnikoff the Nobel Prize for Medicine.

Above The Hoechst Dye Works in the early part of this century. This is where Ehrlich carried out a great deal of his research.

were fraught with danger. A surgeon was obviously the right person to do it. So, as Fleming was a surgeon, he was the one to take it up. Fleming also had no private practice to lose or reputation to ruin if anything went wrong.

But the drug was successful in the treatment of syphilis and further developments in the same series were even more so. Immediately it was tried on all sorts of other illnesses, but of those occurring in our climate none were cured by it.

Wright was not unduly worried by this success. Here was only a single exception to his rule about stimulating immunity being the only right way to cure or prevent disease. But for Fleming it was something to think about. However his chief might explain it away, the Old Man had been shown to be wrong. A chemical *could* work effectively—and safely—inside the body.

3 Interlude: The First World War

War broke out in August 1914. By this time Wright's vaccines were being used against typhoid fever, which in the Boer War had been responsible for more casualties than all the bullets of the Boer farmers. Vaccines were also being used against a number of other diseases with great success. In fact, Wright's typhoid vaccine was so successful (in the First World War only 0.24% of British soldiers caught typhoid compared to over 10% during the Boer War) that after

Below The visit of a doctor to a Boer farm to inoculate the African servants.

the war he was knighted for his efforts and persistance in pressing for its use.

In 1914, however, the War Office decided it did not need any bacteriologists—only ordinary doctors. Wright's team was disbanded and, as they were mostly ex-officers or else, like Fleming and Freeman, territorials, they were sent into the army as battalion medical officers.

It soon became clear that the bacteria were working for the enemy. Infection was killing the wounded in hospitals by the hundred. Gas gangrene and tetanus were responsible for perhaps as much as ten per cent of all the deaths. The old team were recalled. Wright, given the rank of colonel, was sent out to Boulogne to set up a new unit for the study of war wounds. Captain Douglas and Fleming, now a lieutenant, went with him and Leonard Colebrook followed on later. John Freeman was sent first to Russia to prepare cholera vaccines, and afterwards on to Boulogne. The research centre was set up at the Casino and established as the 13th General Hospital. They had as their liaison officer a Frenchman, André Maurois, who described them in *The Silences of Colonel Bramble* and a number of other books. Years later he became Fleming's official biographer.

Again, Wright's group worked as a team and their publications were joint ones. Their experiences must have been horrifying and had a profound effect. They were a fairly tough bunch, used to examining dead bodies in the post-mortem room, but they would never talk about what they went through in Boulogne nor did they ever use their experiences there to illustrate their teaching. Fleming and Colebrook never stopped working on infection, burns and wounds for the rest of their lives.

It was at Boulogne that Fleming conducted a series of brilliant experiments which showed that antiseptic chemicals, when wrongly used, could be dangerous or were, at the very best, useless in fighting infection.

36

Surgeons since the time of Lister had been very enthusiastic about antiseptics and their use spread from surgery to general hospital sterilization and even to the dressing of wounds. All this had become standard teaching—conventional wisdom. 'I remember," Fleming said, "that I used to be told to be most careful to use antiseptics in the dressing of wounds—carbolic acid, boric acid, peroxide of hydrogen. I could see for myself that these antiseptics did not kill all the microbes, but was told that they killed some, and that the results were better than if no antiseptics had been used at all. At that time I was in no position to argue."

What Fleming's experiments at the Casino showed, however, was that not only did some antiseptics that he used fail to attack infections like gangrene, but they actually made things worse! If he put antiseptic chemicals into a wound, into blood or pus, they would kill off the defending white cells more than the invading germs. There was only one chemical that did not do more harm than good. This was known as Eusol (Edinburgh University Solution). This is a hypochlorite solution, and it is sold today as household bleach, in disinfectants for water supplies, for sterilizing babies' bottles and for many other antiseptic uses. As far as Wright was concerned all chemicals for killing bacteria were a failure inside the body. Their place was, precisely, in drains and sinks and Fleming's experiments confirmed this view.

It had become—and still is—normal practice in surgery to use "no-touch" techniques, carefully to avoid contamination and to sterilize everything used during an operation if there is to be any hope of a clean, germ-free result. This is known as *asepsis*, and no matter how clever chemists may become its value should never be forgotten. But the very success in surgery and hospital medicine of both asepsis and antisepsis became a barrier to further progress, and herein lies a lesson. As soon as a scientific idea is

The bacteriology laboratory in which Alexander Fleming worked in the Casino at Boulogne during the First World War. The photograph was taken in October 1916.

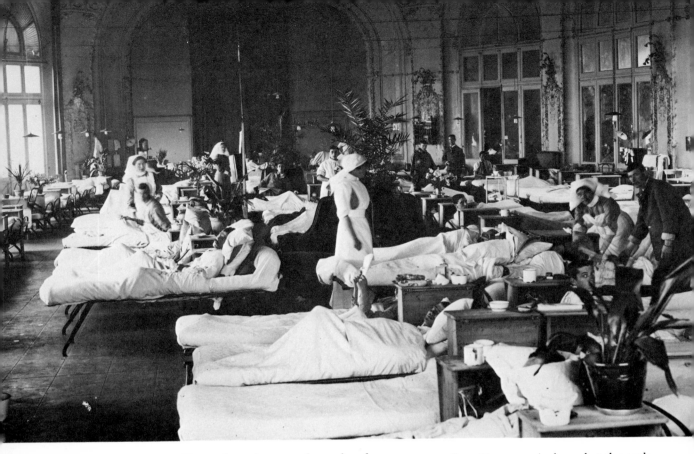

accepted automatically and no longer thought about it becomes as dangerous as a superstition.

Once the war was over the group was brought back together again at St. Mary's Hospital, Paddington. Before the war they had been totally under Wright's control, working on the problems that interested him. Now they were experienced men looking for a chance to follow up their own ideas. But Wright still needed them round him and places had to be found for each of them—rather like major planets with the Old Man himself, Professor Sir Almroth E. Wright, as the sun around which they all moved.

His old friend Captain Douglas presented no problems. He went as director to the Medical Research Council's laboratories. The rest of them had to set up their own lines of research. John Freeman went into practice as an allergist and supported

Above No. 3 surgical ward at the 13th General Hospital, Boulogne during the First World War. This hospital was set up in the Casino and also housed Almroth Wright's team of bacteriologists.

Right Alexander Fleming in the early 1920s.

research into the subject largely out of his own pocket. He built up huge hay-fever and asthma clinics at the hospital. He was from now on constantly played off against his colleague Alexander Fleming with the promise that when Wright retired (a thing he never intended to do anyway), Freeman would be head of the new Institute that Wright had founded.

The income of the Institute, like the Pasteur and Lister Institutes depended on the sale of its vaccines, and this became Fleming's territory. An American firm, Parke Davis, was the only drug house that would market them. The money earned in this way had not only to support research but also to pay for the diagnostic work of the hospital, for the teaching of bacteriology and for the rest of the hospital's work on diseases.

Fleming was also involved on the teaching side and

he had now been given the title of Professor. His new status did not, however, give him any greater control of the funds of the Institute, nor did he find himself more able to influence its policy, but at least he now had a small room of his own (on the turret stairs under the library) and research students to work with him.

Leonard Colebrook worked closely with Wright for a time but he left the department when the chance came to take up full time research as Director of the Bernard Baron Institute at Queen Charlotte's Maternity Hospital. Building up a brilliant research team mainly, though not entirely, drawn from the next generation of St. Mary's students, he set them to work on infections in mothers and babies and brought in safer methods of childbirth. He was, later on, to play a very important part in the development of drugs against bacteria and remained throughout his career on friendly terms with the group at St. Mary's.

Lady Amalia Fleming unveiling a bust of Sir Alexander Fleming in 1956.

4 Lysozyme–Nature's Antiseptic

Although Fleming's day was made up of routine work and teaching, his spare time was now his own and he used it to follow up his own ideas. Up to now he had been very influential in getting people to understand that, in general, chemicals could not be used safely inside the body. Now he was to make one of his great, and apparently casual, observations that was to overthrow this, his own position, and so clear the way for the great advance of antibiotics (anti-bacterial drugs).

Of all bacteriologists at that time, Fleming knew most about the action of antiseptics in the body. Without doubt, he believed, they were harmful. One of them, however, had worked: "606" (salvarsan) and a better version, neosalvarsan.

In the story of the next observation, again something happens that was not planned. Indeed, it could not have been foreseen in any way.

If you look at a portrait or a bust of Fleming you will see that he had an unusual nose. It is part of the Fleming myth that he had broken it either boxing or playing football. As far as I know he did neither of these things and his nose was never in fact broken. In a slightly modified form it has been inherited by his only son Robert. It is just the family nose. However, he did seem to be prone to catarrh and as he always had a cigarette stuck to his lower lip, his nose dripped in cold weather. It was because of this that he covered the top of his microscope with a wash leather guard.

One winter day while he was examining some bacterial colonies growing on a culture plate his nose dripped onto some of them. These colonies had not been planted there by Fleming but had come by accident from the air. They were *contaminants*. The colonies splashed by the mucus melted away; there were others like them on the plate and he was able to *sub-culture* these onto other plates and so build up a supply. This organism which became, and still is, the test for the substance was not known before and his was for many years the only *strain* in the collections. It has now been discovered growing on plant material but it will grow at body temperature or it would not have thrived on Fleming's plates.

At once he set out on a beautiful series of experiments to show where the substance dissolving the bacteria was present in the human body and also how widely it was to be found in nature.

He found it in all the body fluids and in almost every body tissue. He also had the help of the zoo at Regent's Park. When one of their animals died and had a post-mortem examination, various parts of its body were sent to him.

His final conclusion was that this substance, called lysozyme at Wright's suggestion, was an *enzyme*, that is a substance vital to certain bodily chemical changes, and an important part of the body's defences against disease. It is also what keeps eggs free of germs. He published his first paper on lysozyme with his lifelong friend V. D. Allison in 1922 and finally summarized the work in a presidential address to the Pathology Section of the Royal Society of Medicine ten years later. At this meeting he was able to show that the pike's eggs he had used ten years before for his earlier paper were still as active as ever.

He never threw anything away. Thirteen years after, we were trying to get the laboratories tidy after the Second World War. Test tubes, their once white cotton wool plugs black with the dust of the blitz and the soot from Paddington station, were being cleared out of his cupboards. He rescued some from the waste paper baskets saying, "Don't throw them away, they are my pike's eggs and kangaroo tendons." He kept them

Another method of obtaining lysozyme—the antiseptic contained in tears.

until there was an exhibition of work in the laboratory and used them yet again to show that another spell in a test tube in a cupboard had not weakened the enzyme.

The source of lysozyme for his early experiments was human tears. They were clean and easily got by seizing a passing student or laboratory boy and dropping lemon juice in his eye. We now use egg white which has a stronger concentration of lysozyme, and is less painful.

This discovery did not help directly in the treatment of disease. Everyone has enough lysozyme in his body to kill any germ that is affected by it. It has been, however, of great value in dissolving germs so that they can be studied chemically and it is now a standard research tool. The papers Fleming wrote were important in other ways.

For him, and us, the value of this work was twofold—first in method and second in thought. He needed methods that would measure differences in sensitivity to lysozyme of various microbes using only a very small amount of lysozyme. He used a method of diffusion. He made holes, or wells, with a cork borer in the jelly in his culture plates, and filled them with a solution of lysozyme. The various germs to be tested would be spread around the holes. Their sensitivity to lysozyme would be measured by how far away from the hole they were killed. Indeed, almost all the methods we now use in testing antibiotics were developed from Fleming's tests on lysozyme.

Below Fleming's method of measuring how sensitive different bacteria are to lysozyme (or any antiseptic). A hole would be made in the jelly in the culture plates which would then be filled with lysozyme. The germs under scrutiny would be spread in lines around the hole as shown, and their sensitivity would be measured by how far up the line the lysozyme killed the germ.

Perhaps more important was the change in Fleming's thinking about chemicals in the body. He states the case himself in his 1932 presidential address.

"I think I am correct in saying that in 1921 most bacteriologists agreed with the quotation from Metchnikoff:

" 'Nature, to protect the skin and mucous membranes, does not use antiseptics. The fluids which bathe the surface of the mouth and other mucous membranes are not bactericidal, or only very imperfectly so. Nature removes from the mucous membranes and the skin quantities of microbes,

Below A development of Fleming's method for testing the power of antiseptics using a trough instead of a hole.

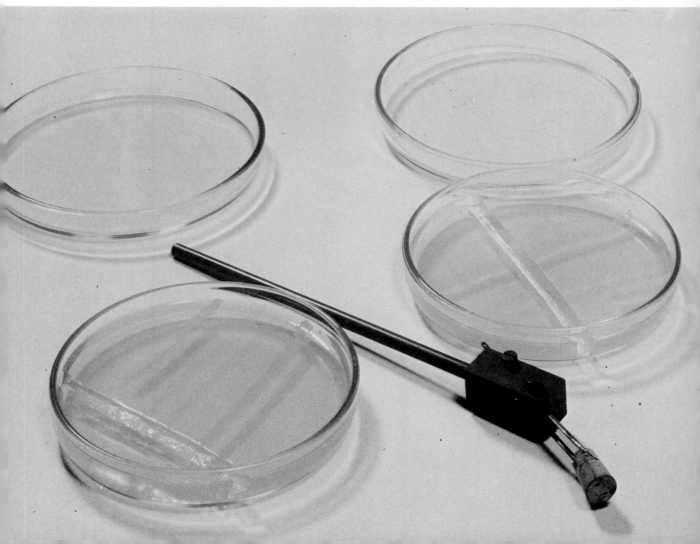

eliminating them by epithelial desquamation and expelling them with the secretions and liquid excretions. Nature has chosen this mechanical procedure. . . .' " (*Epithelial desquamation* means "the flaking-off of skin.")

Fleming then continues with his own comment. "The work which has been done in connection with lysozyme has certainly caused us to modify our views in this respect and has shown that quite apart from phagocytosis and the bactericidal power of the blood fluids, the tissues and secretions have also some primary antiseptic properties."

The term *phagocytosis* which he uses here means the "eating up" of germs by the white cells of the blood. The *bactericidal* power of the fluids is the killing of germs by blood without any white cells taking part. It is clear that Fleming had now arrived at the idea that there might well be chemical substances which would kill bacteria without harming the body's own cells. The idea was not really new as two special examples were already known. Quinine was used against malaria, and salvarsan, as Fleming's own experience had shown, worked well in curing syphilis. Neither of these showed any very bad effects on the patient, though they were by no means perfect. But Fleming, like the other people of his time, had thought of these as odd exceptions.

Fleming now began to accept the general idea of safe chemicals killing germs in the body. This, together with the new techniques he had worked out for testing lysozyme, put him in an ideal position to take advantage of his next observation. Chance was ready to play its trump card.

5 *The Discovery of Penicillin—The Contaminating Mould*

It was September 1928—seven years after lysozyme had been discovered. They had, however, been years of disappointment as far as that was concerned. Fleming was convinced that he had made a discovery of immense importance but his series of superb studies on the matter had raised little excitement in the medical world. But he soon busied himself with new experiments, following up new ideas.

Fleming's laboratory as it was in 1928.

He was now investigating the range of variation in a certain type of bacterium called staphylococcus—trying to find out in what ways individual bacteria of the same type were different from each other. For example, at that time nothing was known about the sex life of bacteria, or even if they had one, and nothing was known about their patterns of heredity. Yet it was clear from slight alterations in colour or shape between different colonies of the same type that not all individuals were alike. These differences seemed important to Fleming. He had managed in earlier experiments to change certain staphylococci in such a way that lysozyme could no longer kill them. How did this happen? Could every single bacterium of this type learn to resist lysozyme or just one or two special bacteria which would then pass on their ability by breeding new population? This was the sort of question Fleming was asking and he was hoping that his new series of experiments might give him some answers.

For this purpose he was breeding a number of different strains of staphylococci. He would from time to time lift the lids of his culture plates to check on how they were getting on. One of them, he noticed one day, had developed a green mould. How annoying! It was now useless. He would have to throw it away. For the moment he just put it to one side with some others that had also been contaminated with various moulds. Tidiness was not one of Fleming's strong points. In those days when culture plates had been finished with they were dropped into a dish full of antiseptic. This would make them safe to handle for whoever washed up. By the time Fleming got round to returning his used dishes, the pile was so high that those on top were well clear of the antiseptic.

On that day, however, Merlin Pryce, who had been helping Fleming with his earlier experiments on variation in bacteria, dropped by to see how things were going. Fleming pointed to some of the plates he

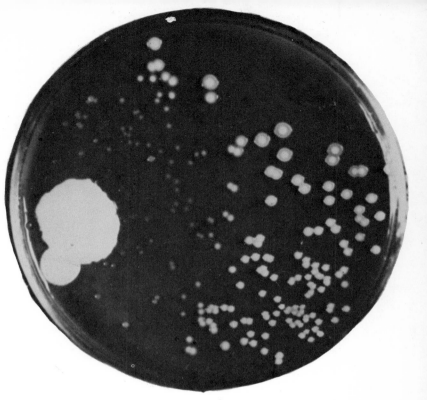

Fleming's original photograph of the
penicillium mould.

had thrown away. "As soon as you uncover a culture
dish something tiresome is sure to happen," he said.
"Things fall out of the air." Then something caught
his eye in the plate with the green mould. All around
the mould the staphylococci colonies had disappeared. Everywhere else in the dish they were
flourishing. The mould was producing something
that was killing the staphylococci.

We now know that the something was penicillin, a
drug that was to revolutionize medicine. But Fleming
did not know that. Though excited by his find, his
experience with antiseptics had made him unusually
cautious. He jumped to no hasty conclusions but went
to work. The arrival of the mould itself may have been
the accident of all accidents, but the next phase was
hard work by a man ideally suited to the job. I believe
that the plate would have been wasted on any other
bacteriologist at the time. Fleming alone was interested in natural antiseptics. He had unique
experience with lysozyme. He tried all his lysozyme

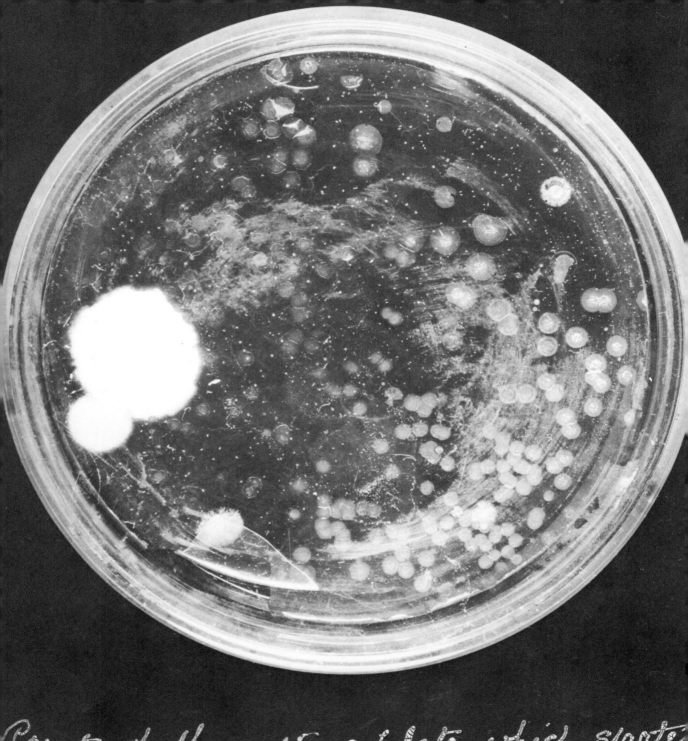

Print of the culture plate which started
the work on Penicillium
(2 years old and rather dried up)

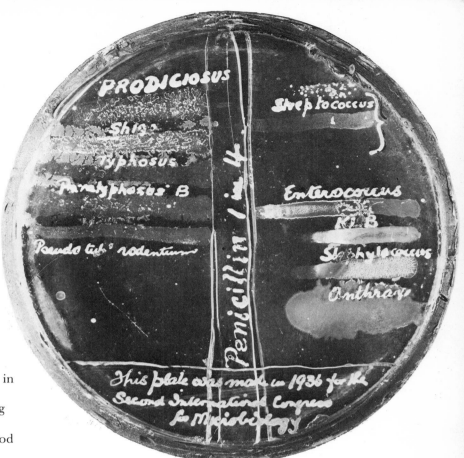

The handwriting on the plate reads:

PRODIGIOSUS

Shig?

Typhosus

Paratyphosus B

Pseudo tub* rodentium

Streptococcus

Enterococcus

N B

Staphylococcus

Anthrax

Penicillin 1 ... H.

This plate was made in 1936 for the Second International Congress for Microbiology

Right A demonstration plate (made in 1936 for the second International Congress of Microbiology) showing the effect of penicillin on various organisms—using the trough method illustrated on page 45.

Left The original plate on which the penicillium mould was first discovered now yellowed with age and used as a demonstration piece. The handwriting is Fleming's.

tricks with the mould juice and they worked perfectly. He tested its effect on a wide range of disease germs, leaving out only two major ones—tetanus and gas gangrene.

Although Fleming now had a steady supply of penicillium cultures he was never able to reproduce the appearance of his original plate. If at any time he wanted to come up with a similar culture for teaching purposes, he had to prepare it another way. He had to "fake" it by growing the mould first (giving it plenty of time to make penicillin) and then planting the staphylococci, growing them for one day. The original plate is still kept but is now just a dried up disk and looks like a piece of old plastic discoloured by being left out in the sun.

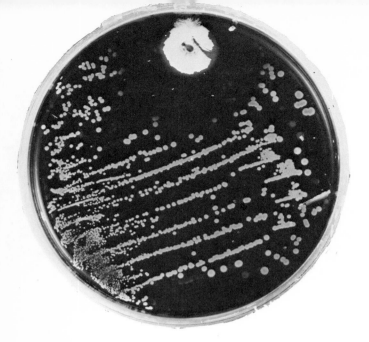

Left The author's reproduction using Hare's method showing that the exact requirements of the original plate have now been met. *Right* Professor Ronald Hare (1899–   ) of St. Thomas's Hospital who worked out the exact conditions under which the original mould appeared.

Professor Ronald Hare of St. Thomas' Hospital was a junior worker in the department at the time that Fleming saw his mould for the first time. Not long ago he worked out the exact conditions that were needed to produce the original plate, and in doing so managed what Fleming had never been able to do.

This story follows Professor Hare's explanation, as told to the History of Medicine Section of the Royal Society of Medicine, of how it came about that the man met his mould.

The staphylococci that Fleming was working on often, but not always, produce a substance that is normally yellow or gold in colour. It varies so much that you could pick off bright orange-yellow at one end of the population and white at the other.

Someone in Belgium published a paper about this subject. He wrote that he found a much better range of colours if the cultures were allowed to develop at room temperature, about 20°C, than if, as is normal, they were grown at body temperature, 37°C. So Fleming tried it for a few weeks. They were vital weeks for all of us.

His own story of the discovery is short. It reads:

"While working with staphylococcal variants a number of culture-plates were set aside on the laboratory bench and examined from time to time. In the examination these plates were necessarily exposed to the air and they became contaminated with various micro-organisms. It was noticed that around a large colony of contaminating mould the staphylococcus colonies became transparent and were obviously undergoing lysis."

How did the mould arrive there? It so happened that off the staircase in the turret where Fleming worked there were a number of rooms similar to his. The one immediately underneath was occupied by a mycologist called La Touche. A mycologist is a specialist in moulds and fungi of all sorts from toadstools right down to cells not much larger than bacteria.

He had been brought into the department by John Freeman. Freeman had originally been interested in hay-fever and asthma due to grass pollen. His attention had now turned to "dust asthma," which he thought might be due to mould spores in damp houses. For his researches he wanted a large bulk of mould spores from his patients' own homes. With these he made extracts for testing on their skin.

Mycologists at that time were not used to handling organisms that were known to cause disease in man. They were less careful in their methods and did not feel worried if some of the spore cultures were spilled or shaken into the air. There were probably more mould spores in the air of St. Mary's laboratories at that time than ever before or since. It is more likely that the famous mould arrived that way than that it was blown through the windows as the usual story suggests. Bacteriologists do not work with open windows. Certainly Fleming never did. His window had a particularly stiff sash and could only be reached by leaning over the bench where there was a bunsen burner and several hot water baths.

Fleming believed that the mould got onto his plate when he lifted its lid to look at it. This is probably not true for a number of reasons. Most important is that the mould does not start to produce penicillin straight away. Only when it has developed into a fairly large colony do the drops of yellow fluid begin to appear on the surface and spread over the culture plate or into the flask of broth—and this takes about five days. Penicillin acts on bacterial cell walls in such a way that it only works while the bacteria (staphylococci in this case) are still growing. After growth has stopped, the bacteria cannot be killed.

The staphylococci that Fleming was growing normally stopped dividing in about eighteen hours, at 37°C in an incubator. If he had not been growing them on a bench, a slower business all together, the mould juice would not have killed them. They had still to be growing after five days. An incubator can be controlled, but growing at room temperature depends on the weather. The mould and the organism each had to grow at just the right rate, which happened to be about 18°C. It was vital that the temperature did not rise above this for nearly a week. It was the first week in August and unusually chilly for that time of year, and the temperature did not, incredibly, rise above that critical 18°C (60°F).

Already we have a series of accidents all of which had to happen together to make the discovery possible. Out of all the moulds that occur in nature, how many of them would have produced the effect he saw? Years later, after the Second World War, drug houses in many countries started a search for moulds in all sorts of places: the fruit markets of the southern states of the U.S.A., the forest floor in Central America, the sewage outflow of Mediterranean islands. It is guessed that at least a million had to be examined before a new and useful one was found. This would confirm the theory that the mould came from La

A cartoon illustrating Ronald Hare's theory of the origin of Fleming's penicillium mould.

"It was here Sir Alexander Fleming discovered penicillin."

Touche's downstairs laboratory. Fleming wrote that La Touche found him four more strains of penicillium that did the same thing. This must mean that he had plenty of material there. The strains could even have all come from the same house.

Were Fleming's colleagues and the other bacteriologists in the country enthusiastic about his discovery? They were not!

The first report was given to the Medical Research Club. This was a private group which held informal after dinner meetings. They showed no interest whatsoever and did not even discuss it at any length as far as we can find out. The club members probably dismissed it as another of Fleming's pretty experiments on antibacterial substances.

It must have been for him a nightmarish occasion. His audience was, and still is, one of the most exacting. He was such a very unattractive speaker that it is easy to understand why they were not impressed. It must have been quite an ordeal for the shyest man I ever met.

His great paper was published in a research journal, *The British Journal of Experimental Pathology*. This journal publishes quickly and accepts unusual papers. It has the drawback that its readership consists of other research workers and not clinicians, that is doctors working directly with patients. Nowadays such a paper would also be reported in a short form, an abstract, in journals which specialize in this; then none existed.

His title was enough to put off any casual reader. It was "On the Antibacterial Action of Cultures of a Penicillium, with special reference to their use in the isolation of B. influenzae." Now why did he call it that? Well, finding a title for a paper that makes ten points is not easy.

Fleming settled for facts for which he could show an immediate, practical laboratory use; he was not prepared to speculate, to daydream, to claim

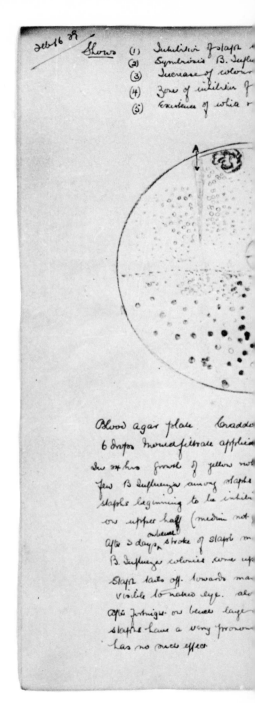

A page from Fleming's bench notes dated Feb. 16 '29.

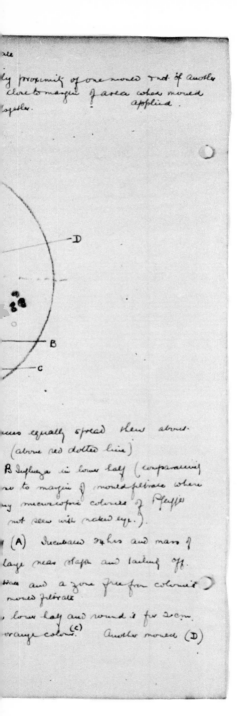

anything that he could not fully prove. But he certainly saw the possibilities of the mould juice.

It is worth looking at a summary of this paper:

1. A certain type of penicillium mould produces, when cultured, a powerful substance that kills bacteria. This antibacterial power reaches its maximum in about seven days when grown at 20°C and after ten days starts to get less and less until it has almost disappeared after four weeks.

2. The growth medium which has best produced the antibacterial substance is ordinary nutrient broth.

3. The active ingredient can be filtered off easily and the name "penicillin" has been given to it.

4. The action is very marked against the pus-forming bacteria and the diphtheria group of bacilli. Many bacteria, however, are quite insensitive to it.

5. Penicillin is not poisonous to animals, even in enormous doses, nor is it an irritant. It does not interfere with the action of the white cells in the blood.

6. It is suggested that it may be a good antiseptic to use against penicillin-sensitive microbes in the body.

7. The use of penicillin on culture plates brings to light the way in which bacteria may interfere with others. This is not very evident in ordinary cultures.

8. The value of penicillin isolating *B. influenzae* (a type of 'flu germ) has been demonstrated.

It is all there in that one paper. In the face of this, to say Fleming did not see the uses (and the limitations) of the drug is obviously wrong.

With all this to select from, and probably having heard his report to the club as well, Topley and Wilson, the authors of the great text book of bacteriology, merely wrote in their next edition that penicillin was the juice of a mould said by Fleming to be useful in isolating *B. influenzae*. We may take this to be the official view of the time.

A large scale magnification of the penicillium fungus.

6 *The Period of Failure and Neglect*

Fleming had made an important observation and worked out methods for culturing the penicillium mould. Obviously, his next step should have been to get hold of large amounts to continue experiments with laboratory animals and then with human patients. Why did he not do this? The answer is that penicillin is an unstable substance. It very quickly goes off. At that time there were no chemical methods which could deal with such unstable substances. It was not because Fleming and his assistants did not want to isolate it, not because they did not try hard; it was just that it was too soon. Chemistry and chemical techniques had not progressed enough to make it possible.

A number of things had to happen before penicillin could be made in useful amounts. The first was that the medical profession as a whole had to be persuaded to change its mind about the use of drugs in infection. The second was that new techniques in biochemistry had to be introduced into this country. What finally did the trick was that a situation arose which made the government want penicillin so badly that it was ready to spend a lot of money to get it.

Fleming first of all tried to get Wright to put up the money for the chemical research which would be needed to develop penicillin. But Wright was rather against chemists. He thought them inhuman and he hated to think that, one day, the active ingredients of blood which were responsible for immunity might be seen to be chemical substances. He insisted on thinking of them as "functions" of the blood. Nowadays they are known, and measured, chemically. Most of them are what are called globulins.

Above left Frederick Ridley
(1903–   ) and *above* Stuart Craddock (1904–1972), who made early,
but unsuccessful, attempts at
preparing penicillin in a stable form.

There were no proper chemists in the department and none, even among the medical school's chemistry teachers, who could, or would, attempt to prepare pure penicillin. The only help that could be found was given by two young men, Frederick Ridley and Stuart Craddock, who had some chemical knowledge. They were given a sink and draining board in a corridor just outside the laboratory. Their studies almost led to a stable preparation but the final step was beyond them.

When they had done their best and failed, Fleming tried to get help from other laboratories in the University of London. These again failed either because the chemists got no help from their own bacteriologists, or because there was no real enthusiasm.

So at this stage Fleming was left with another substance which, like lysozyme, had no clinical uses. Many years later, Fleming said, "I had failed for want of adequate chemical help. Raistrick and his

Above Professor Harold Raistrick (1890–1971) of the London School of Hygiene and Tropical Medicine, who also spent a good deal of time trying to get penicillin in a pure and stable form. His team had only a limited success. They found that penicillin could be extracted from the culture fluid but most of it was destroyed in the process.

associates had lacked bacteriological cooperation." Professor Harold Raistrick was at the School of Tropical Medicine and Hygiene. He had spent some time investigating penicillin but his efforts to get it in its pure form had only limited success.

So, for the next six years, Fleming and his mould were forgotten. He wrote a few articles for text books but published little that was new. We know, of course, what he was doing at this time but his work on penicillin had to be shelved. Penicillin had to wait for other men to make it famous.

Fleming's time was taken up with the usual duties of a professor. He did some organizing, some teaching and some diagnostic work for hospital patients as well as his own outpatients. Apart from these routine duties he spent a lot of his time testing and improving the department's vaccines. This was a special interest of his for the whole research programme now depended on the sale of these vaccines.

Another of Fleming's interests during this period was in the way in which one type of living microbe interferes with others. He did a great deal of work to find out how one particular germ could be selected for study by suppressing others that were in its company. For this he took advantage of his knowledge of resistance and sensitivity to penicillin and crude chemicals such as the dyes. He was not alone in this. The modern methods of selection on which so much present day diagnosis depends were the result of a broad advance by his colleagues all over the world.

The sort of problem that interference between microbes caused can be illustrated by an outbreak of diptheria in a certain boys' school. At the same time as the diphtheria bacillus was going round the school there was also a staphylococcus. In those boys with diphtheria alone, the diagnosis was made immediately but in those with both germs it was missed. Why? The reason is that when the two germs were put together on a culture plate, the staphylococcus stopped the bacillus growing. A missed diagnosis like this would not happen today. All laboratories now use the selective plates developed by bacteriologists in the 1930s.

At this time Fleming did his own reputation no good. He never liked to blow up an observation or experiment into a published paper. He far preferred to make his points by pretty little demonstrations at laboratory meetings. He presented the results of his work on microbe selection by making drawings on filter paper with a mixture of differently coloured bacteria. If the filter paper turned out to be yellow, this meant that the yellow bacteria were stopping the others growing. When he dripped onto the filter paper a chemical which killed only the yellow bacteria red or purple ones would grow in their place. This was meant to put an important point simply and visually. Instead, his critics saw it only as a game with bacteria and nothing else.

The scale of the work had, by now, grown enormously. The Institute moved out of the disused hospital wards into a specially built suite of laboratories next to the new medical school. Here Fleming had a number of assistants who were loyal to him, rather than to the older generation represented by Wright. It is interesting that most of them were at least half Scottish and were all short men. Much of the stimulus and many of the ideas for their work came from Fleming, but, unlike the traditional continental professor, he did not ask for his name to appear on the papers they wrote. He did not, then, or at any time, search for fame or publicity. Before he would let anything be published it had to be up to the standard he required. But then, as long as it was known to come from the department, he did not look for any credit for himself. He explained his attitude to me when he was eventually Head of the Institute. It was clearly a direct reaction to Wright's position. He had been trained on the continent and it was the

Below Leonard Colebrook (1883–1967) as a young man at St. Mary's Hospital. Colebrook, one of Wright's team before and during the First World War, moved after the war to Queen Charlotte's Maternity Hospital where he made great advances in the treatment of puerperal fever.

fashion there for the head of a department to be mentioned in everything that his department published.

Fleming pointed out that our "tea parties" were for the exchange of ideas. These could be thrown into the conversation by anyone. They were tossed from one person to another, improved and altered to appear finally in a form which suggested an experiment. Fleming insisted that the credit should not go to the person who had the first idea, or started the conversation, but to whoever did the hard bench work to prove or disprove it. The only drawback of this system is that you cannot tell who had the ideas and who was merely a good routine worker.

Over this period the whole attitude to chemotherapy, that is to the drug treatment of infections, was coming round to Fleming's viewpoint. This change was brought about not by him, but by his old friend Leonard Colebrook at Queen Charlotte's

Below right Leonard Colebrook using an air sampler at Birmingham Accident Hospital where he worked from 1943 to 1951.

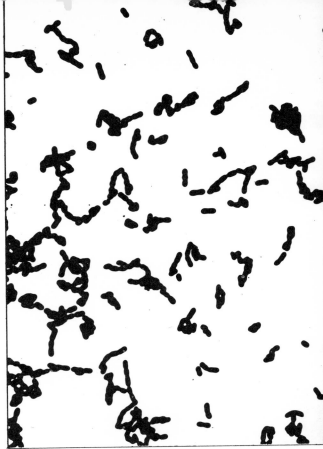

Maternity Hospital. Colebrook had been working with a small but brilliant team on infection in women who had had babies. This disease, puerperal fever, is a form of blood poisoning by bacteria. Up to one in ten mothers who came into hospital to have their babies caught it and many died every year.

The bacteria which cause this disease are streptococci, round or oval germs arranged like beads on a thread. Colebrook's attention was drawn to a German paper which suggested that a red dye, prontosil, could cure mice of streptococcal infections. Might this work on the sick mothers? First he showed that it *was* successful in killing the streptococci causing the disease. It was then found out that the dye itself was not needed, only a certain colourless ingredient. This was just as well. It stopped everything about the patient being stained bright red!

Above left Staphylococci growing in typical grape-like clusters. In the preparation of the film some of the clusters have broken up as they always do. You can see an occasional coccus by itself. *Above* Streptococci showing their tendency to grow in chains. Each photograph shows bacteria at 1,000 times magnification.

Above The Sir William Dunn School of Pathology where Howard Florey and Ernst Chain carried out their research into penicillin around the beginning of the Second World War.

This ingredient, suphanilamide, turned out to be the first good drug that could be used in medicine since salvarsan twenty-five years before.

Colebrook called on Fleming, who knew all the techniques, and asked him to find out how sulphanilamide worked. Fleming discovered that it did no harm to blood cells, but, a most interesting fact, it could not kill germs without them. It stopped the germs from multiplying, but the white cells of the blood had to do the killing.

This new chemical and others that were soon made from it changed the whole thinking of doctors in our country. At last they were ready to consider other possible killers of bacteria. The stage was now set for the second entrance of penicillin. To trace penicillin's reemergence we have to go up the line from Paddington to Oxford to meet a refugee from Hitler's

Germany, a young chemist called Ernst Chain.

Oxford University had recently appointed a keen young Australian as Professor of Pathology. His name was Howard Florey. He believed that bacteriology needed chemists to complete the work started by the bacteriologists, so he was soon on the lookout for a biochemist. He went for help and advice to Professor Gowland Hopkins at Cambridge, whose department was putting up some refugees from Germany. Chain was introduced to Florey and joined his team.

Florey quickly followed up his idea of the need for chemical skill in bacteriology. He sent out everyone he could find, including the medical students, to hunt through library books to find any incomplete work that was worth pushing further. Chain started work with a young bacteriologist called Duthie. He worked first on chemicals produced by the body during inflammation. After that, he investigated lysozyme and showed that it was in fact an enzyme. His third substance was penicillin.

Chain used the published results of Fleming and his team and added his own chemical knowledge. He had no difficulty in producing a dry brown powder that did not lose its power after a few days.

On the morning of Saturday, 25th May, 1940, Florey tested the powder on four white Swiss albino mice which he had infected with streptococci. Four more he infected in the same way, but these he did not treat with the penicillin that Chain had so carefully prepared. By three o'clock the next morning, all four of the second batch of mice were dead. All four which had been given penicillin, however, were still alive. Florey and Chain were thrilled (Chain was almost dancing with excitement). They immediately made plans for more experiments, and for increasing the production of penicillin by all possible means.

The results of Florey and Chain's experiments were published in August, 1940, in *The Lancet*. The paper

Dr. Ernst Chain (1906–   ), the German-born chemist who fled to Britain in 1933 and who successfully prepared penicillin in a stable form and with Fleming and Florey shared the Nobel Prize for Medicine in 1945 for his part in its development.

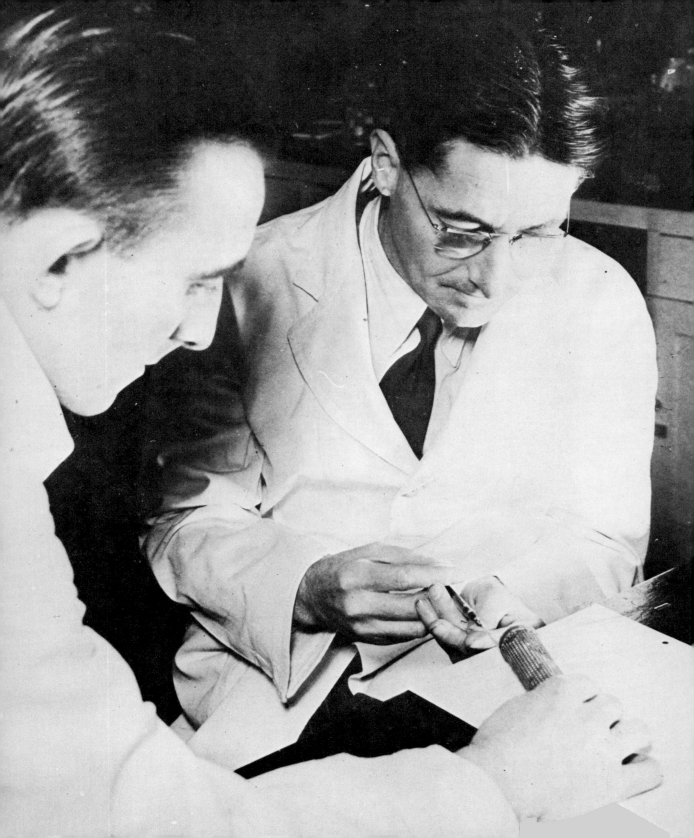

Left Howard Walter Florey (1898–1968), the Australian-born pathologist, injecting a mouse with penicillin. His assistant, J. H. D. Kent, is holding the mouse container. Florey was Professor of Pathology at Oxford from 1935 to 1962.

Above Penicillin was originally produced in commercial quantities by the method of surface culture of the mould.

was entitled "Penicillin as a Chemotherapeutic Agent." At the time, Chain did not know that Fleming was still alive. But he was.

He was delighted at this new interest in his discovery, even when all the public credit was given to the Oxford team with no mention of Fleming. Wright, however, would not stand for one of his own people being overlooked in this way, even though he did not like the chemical approach. He wrote a letter to *The Times*, in which he put the matter right and made it quite clear where the original work had been done.

Oxford has never quite adjusted to this and there has for many years been a plaque in the memorial rose garden outside the Physic Garden which credits Florey and Chain with the entire discovery of penicillin's clinical importance, no credit at all being given to Fleming.

It is worth thinking about and comparing Fleming's and the Oxford team's contribution towards giving the world penicillin. It tells us something about the way that scientific knowledge increases today. With men like Louis Pasteur, Edward Jenner and Joseph Lister, the great discoveries were the result of one man's efforts in following up what was often chance observation. Since then, the trend has been towards groups of research workers, no one of whom could claim all the credit for a discovery or its development. Their research is often a planned investigation of a chosen field.

Fleming's own description of himself as a Victorian naturalist with a modern microscope of course ignores his skill at investigating and exploring the things he came on. Chain, on this occasion, was acting as a skilled chemist using his special knowledge on an existing problem—how to make a penicillin extract that would not be destroyed quickly on keeping. But lucky observations were not now a thing of the past. Chain himself was able to make one. He showed this when he was trying to grow a disease of rye, the fungus ergot, which is also a source of important drugs. However hard he tried he just could not find a strain that would grow in deep broth cultures. One Sunday afternoon he recognized the symptoms of the disease in some rye grass growing by the side of a picnic spot where he was with his family. This gave him the culture he needed.

The small "penicillin factory" at the
Sir William Dunn School of
Pathology in 1941 or 1942.

7 Penicillin and the Second World War

Fleming's reaction to the new situation was at once to place the resources of St. Mary's Hospital at the disposal of the Oxford team.

We had a factory on the third floor of the building and in the basement, where vaccines were being produced for the Forces. We had the means of growing larger amounts of mould than Oxford could and our technicians had been making it every week since its discovery. The penicillin in its crude form in broth was poured off into large churns and put on to the passenger trains at Paddington to be collected at Oxford only about an hour later by their technicians.

This help was fully repaid when a very small amount of penicillin was being produced for clinical use. Florey let Fleming have the whole of his stock to treat a friend of his with a brain infection. This was the first time penicillin had been injected into the spine. The first civilian patient whose life was saved by penicillin treatment given by Fleming was a police sergeant injured in the blitz!

Fleming was able to draw government attention to penicillin here, as on the Committee of the Institute were the Minister of Supply and an important industrialist. He was the wrong sort of person to influence government departments directly. Florey, on the other hand, had the right approach and succeeded in obtaining official American support.

It was decided that production should be out of reach of the bombs which were then falling on British industrial towns, and hence that the bulk of penicillin production should be carried out in America. Curiously, the people who had the necessary skills

A stage in the modern mass production of penicillin at the Pfizer plant in Groton, U.S.A. It was found that producing penicillin by surface culture was rather clumsy and uneconomical. It is now produced "in suspension"—inside the mould broth. This illustration shows the large filter press which filters off the penicillin crystals from the mould broth which produces them.

were the brewers, and this is why some firms that started out making beer and lager became, and still are, drug houses.

This brings up the question of patents. Humiliating as it was, Britain was having to pay Americans for the rights of production of a British discovery.

One of the great points in British medical ethics has always been that there should be no secret remedies. The term "patent medicine" was almost a term of abuse and was usually taken to mean something dishonest or useless. When Colebrook and his team isolated sulphanilamide, they could have obtained a basic patent for their research institution but, if the idea had ever entered his head, it would have been turned down as quite unethical.

Stages in the production of penicillin: *above* after filtering, washing and drying, the penicillin, now in powder form is removed and must be ground to a constant size of particle for use in injections and filling capsules; *top right* penicillin powder being fed into the grinding mill (in the right of the picture): *bottom right* inspection of penicillin packaging before being sent out to hospitals and drug stores.

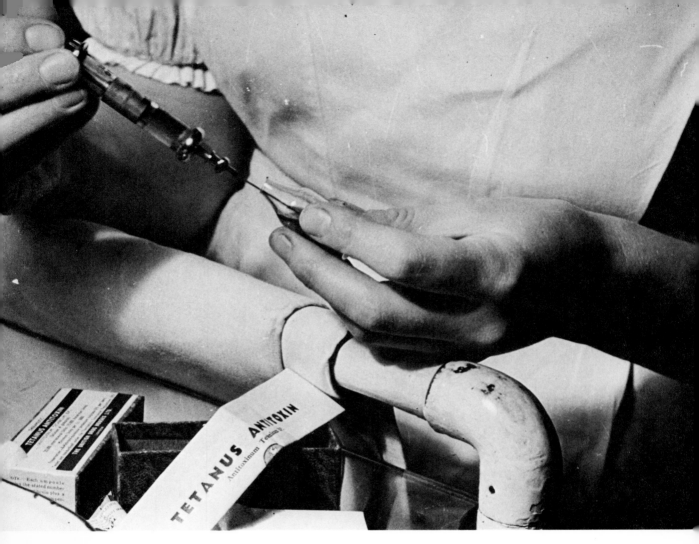

In the same way, none of St. Mary's' vaccines had any secrets about them and anyone could copy them. Only the brand names were protected. Neither Oxford nor St. Mary's gained any financial advantage from their discoveries.

As a result of such unhappy experiences the British Government arranged to hold patents on any discoveries made in universities and similar places. Oxford, for example, gets patent payments on a group of antibiotics called cephalosporins, developed by the same team—but that was not to come about for another twenty years.

Above A syringe being filled with tetanus antitoxin at Guy's Hospital during the Second World War when it became standard practice to give each casualty that came in. The antitoxin is an antidote to bacterial poisons. If the casualty had already received an inoculation with tetanus toxoid, such as produced at this time at St. Mary's Hospital, his own body would have already produced the antitoxins needed.

The war naturally took up the scientific resources at St. Mary's and all the university departments. Fleming was responsible, as Deputy Director, for the supervision of vaccine production. The small "factory" at St. Mary's had produced enough tetanus toxoid to immunize, through the Red Cross organization, both sides in the Spanish Civil War. Tetanus toxin is the poison made by the bacteria that cause tetanus. It is altered to a harmless form called a toxoid, for immunization. This showed that that particular tragedy of the First World War could be avoided. The factory was now expanded to produce in addition to tetanus toxoid, injections against typhoid and cholera, diphtheria, whooping cough and influenza, in case another world epidemic like the one following the First World War should happen again.

Fleming's next responsibility was as sector pathologist. Southern England was divided into ten areas, like slices of a cake, the sharp point of each slice being at a London teaching hospital. Fleming's sector stretched from Paddington along the roads and railways running westwards to Basingstoke, Winchester and Southampton.

Pathologists were sent to set up laboratories to serve these areas and to look after the air raid casualties as they occurred, and later, turning the sectors round, to accept casualties straight from the invasion beaches of Europe on and after D-day.

The war did not go at all as expected and the population of London stayed put. This meant that the central London hospitals had to be reopened not just as casualty clearing stations as had been planned, but with proper outpatient departments and wards to deal with ordinary illness and injury. Half the students were brought back to the hospitals to help with the work there, acting not only as dressers as they normally did, but also as stretcher bearers, fire watchers and unqualified house officers. They still needed teaching and courses were run at the safe provincial hospitals as well as the far from safe London ones by staffs that were already working flat out on emergency services.

There was a committee of sector pathologists, whose job was not only to run the service but also to provide up-to-date advice on all aspects of laboratory work for pathologists in the Armed Services, the Emergency Medical Service and the Public Health Laboratory Service. Here Fleming's skill at the bench and his Scottish thriftiness fitted in with the needs of the time. Methods and results that in peacetime would have been given full scale publication were just thrown out in news sheets and became known everywhere long before they were properly published. I doubt whether Fleming or any of the others will ever get full credit for this part of their work.

It was under these sorts of condition that the standard antibiotic disc, for showing whether a germ is sensitive before the patient is given any drugs, was invented. It is now the standard method and is used all over the world to give a quick guide to treatment.

I was responsible in my part of the sector, for sharing out the very small amounts of penicillin that were issued to civilians. By modern standards, it was a pitifully small amount—about a million units a month for an area with 250,000 people in it. We now give that amount to one person in one day. My fear was that some of it might be wasted by treating patients whose infection was due to germs against which penicillin was useless or germs that could be treated in some other way. If that happened, we might be faced at the end of the month with a patient who could be saved only by penicillin and find ourselves out of stock.

I explained the point to Fleming. He sent me off to get hold of a paper punch which he used to cut discs out of some blotting paper on his bench. He handed them to me and suggested that, having cultured the offending germ, I should put two of them on each

Above The original punch which Fleming used when he thought up his economical method of testing the sensitivity of a particular germ to penicillin.

culture plate. One would contain a single unit of penicillin and the second, ten units. I would then be able to judge the sensitivity of the culture by seeing what effect each disc had on the surrounding germ colonies. The method was reported in the sector pathologist's news sheet.

As soon as it had been tidied up by two of his ex-service trainees at the end of the war, it was published and became one of the standard methods. The size, thickness and source of the discs today are the same as those that came from the original punch. Of course Fleming got no credit for this. He did not expect any. For him, it was a trivial idea. Many of his little laboratory tricks were written up and made more impressive by other people. They appeared as papers and even as theses for higher degrees. This business of starting off an idea and then giving it away to anyone who wanted it was typical of him.

8 Recognition at Last

Fleming and Florey were both knighted in June, 1944. For a short while we did not know quite what to call him. In the end it was "Sir Alexander" behind his back or to visitors but "Flem" still fitted better when you were talking to him.

The greatest possible honour came to him when with Florey and Chain he shared the Nobel Prize for Medicine in 1945.

In the Nobel Lecture which he gave he said, referring to the large scale production of penicillin which he had seen in America, "to me it was of especial interest to see how a simple observation made in a hospital bacteriological laboratory in London had eventually developed into a large industry, and how what everyone thought was merely one of my toys had, by purification, become the nearest approach to the ideal substance for curing many of our common infections."

Fleming himself expected that many more antibiotics would be found and that some of them would turn out to be better than his own.

Some years later, the Japanese discoverer of kanamycin, H. Umezawa, was being entertained in London. He said to me, "It really was not fair for Fleming to find the first and for it still to be the best!"

The situation at the department was still not a completely happy one. Wright had kept power and the control of the research funds very largely in his own hands. He was now an elderly man. Both of his most likely successors, Fleming and Freeman, were themselves nearing retirement. They had been played off against one another and each had been promised that he eventually would take control. The announce-

Fleming's Nobel Prize Medal.

ment of Fleming's knighthood had settled that issue. On that day there was tea as usual in the library. Very few of the old staff were still around—only those who had been called in to help with the clinics, teaching and vaccine production. They joined Wright at tea. He was unusually silent. Fleming came in and sat down. Not a word was said. The secretary came in with a bundle of papers, mainly to do with the vaccine business, and held them out to Wright. He waved them away saying, "Dr. Fleming will deal with them. They are too unimportant for me."

Sir Alexander Fleming being interviewed for Canadian radio in 1947 by Bernard Braden, the famous television personality who was then a radio producer for the Canadian Broadcasting Corporation.

Fleming had by then been a professor for twenty years and his knighthood had been announced in *The Times* that day. This was the Old Man's last gesture as power finally slipped from him, after over forty years of absolute supremacy. Fleming took the papers and went out, still without speaking. It seemed a pity that Wright could not have made some sort of gesture as generous as his letter to *The Times*, a pity that he had to behave so peevishly at the end of his career.

Fleming was now very near the retiring age for professors. It seemed natural that he should become Director of the department, which was now renamed the Wright-Fleming Institute. A new full time professor and staff were appointed as soon as men were released from the Armed Forces and the Emergency Medical Service. These people would deal with all the routine jobs that he hated, and he, Fleming, would be able to concentrate the rest of his time on teaching postgraduates and doing his own research work.

With the ending of the war in Europe, the London hospitals reopened fully and a Medical Research Council unit was set up to study patients being treated with antibiotics. Just as salvarsan was sent to Wright for trial, so now new antibiotics came to Fleming. This time, though, the tragedies of the early days did not recur; none of the workers died, but still far too many developed tuberculosis—the main disease under study. Such experiences at the Institute gave rise to many of the safety precautions now standard in modern laboratories. There were, for example, no protective cabinets to work in. The cultures of tubercle bacilli were tested in test tubes on the open bench. Almost everyone working there had to go at some time or another to a sanatorium for treatment.

This was a time of triumph for Fleming and he was invited to many countries as a hero. Yet he was still a very poor public speaker and people who went to listen to him were usually disappointed. He was hap-

Above Sir Alexander Fleming being
chaired shoulder high by the students
of Edinburgh University after being
installed there as the new Rector in
1952.

Above The Papal Medal awarded to Fleming.

The mould
that first made
Penicillin
Alexander Fleming

piest in the U.S.A. and in Spain. His deadpan delivery and a certain sharp wit in his short replies to newspaper men went down very well in the States, while in Spain he spoke in English and, as his speeches were translated, they sounded much less flat. For some reason the Spanish were quicker to honour him and were more generous towards him than any other people. He collected honorary degrees and the silk hoods that went with them from many places but it was a Spanish one he wore on most ceremonial occasions. This, he said, was because they gave him a hood *and* the gown to go with it!

The Nobel Prize was not the only medal that he was awarded. He also received a number of others, some of them very valuable and beautiful works of art. He showed them to none of his colleagues and the only hospital people to see them were his personal technicians and the joiner in the workshop who made a cabinet for them.

He was not only shy about owning them but he also found receiving them very embarrassing. He thought up a way of getting over this uneasiness. He grew his mould on black paper which could be lifted off the culture medium when growth was complete. The paper discs, about an inch across, were now fixed and dried. They fitted neatly into little glass frames with tortoise-shell backs and a space on which he could write something suitable for the occasion. These frames were made for him by his brother Robert, who was in the optical industry.

One of them came in handy when he went to receive the medal of the Papal Academy of Science from the Pope. When he came back from the plane he was in an almost talkative mood for him. I asked how he got on with the Pope. "Fine! He is a nice little man. He sat on one side of the fireplace and I sat on the other and we talked a bit. Then he pulled this out of his pocket and gave it to me. Not to be outdone I gave him one of mine."

Below the Papal Medal Fleming's medal of the type that he gave the Pope in return.

85

These months, which should have been so happy for him, were spoilt by the tragic illness of his wife. We saw little of her in the department as she had a painful disease of the spine which was quite incurable. They went together to Spain but she became even more seriously ill there, and had to stay in the hotel in Madrid unable to go with him to the special meeting that had been arranged at the universities in Madrid and elsewhere. She came back to England to face a final illness which also affected her mind.

During this last illness Fleming was desolate. He would sit looking into space, doing and saying nothing. Luckily some of his staff were around to give him the only treatment likely to help. We made him do some work. We would set up experiments and take the results to him for checking and interpreting. Our subject for study was the change brought about in bacteria by penicillin and other drugs. One effect of penicillin was to make the bacteria swell up and burst. Somehow it stopped them building strong cell walls, but did not stop them growing. Soon he was so interested that we had him at work again.

Before the first results were published, another fortunate thing happened. As had happened with vaccines in Wright's time, foreign workers now came to the department to learn our latest methods and find out about antibiotics. One of them was a Greek woman doctor who had suffered as a prisoner in a German concentration camp. She came to us as much to give her a chance to relax and regain her strength, as to study and learn. We asked Fleming to let her join our team as the rest of us were heavily committed to our hospital work and had little time for research. He agreed and she worked with us. After a while he was sufficiently recovered and she sufficiently trained for him to take her on as his research assistant, and we could turn to other things.

She spoke four or five European languages and so was particularly helpful in showing foreign visitors

Sir Alexander and Lady Fleming interviewed by the B.B.C. Greek section in 1954.

round and interpreting for them. Later, after Lady Fleming's death, she acted as Fleming's hostess and took from him the strain of entertaining his guests. He missed her very much when her scholarship ended and she had to return to Athens. And it came as no surprise to us that he stopped in Athens on his way back from a tour of India, and later announced that she would be the second Lady Fleming. The marriage lasted a happy two years. In March, 1955, just after he retired from the Institute, Alexander Fleming died of a heart attack.

What, then, can be said finally about this exceedingly shy little man? He deliberately hid the truth about himself. When he was famous all press cuttings about him were sent to his secretary. All the false stories invented by journalists and others were collected in a special file to make up what we called the "Fleming Myth." He would tell all these stories at dinner parties with a perfectly straight face. The more unlikely they were the more they appealed to him. They let the real man hide away, and this is what he seemed to want.

Was he a genius? The *Daily Mirror* described him as one in a two page article. I took it in to him and asked what you had to do to be a genius. After a long pause he said, "You've got to be lucky." Oddly enough, I heard Ernst Chain suggest the same thing, only he said, "You've got to be lucky twice."

This is the story of the Fleming I knew in the laboratory. The other sides to his life, and what he wrote and said, can be found in his official biography.

His work was marked by certain qualities. He devoted himself entirely to his day to day job. To this he brought a very clever hand and a watching eye. Whenever he saw something unusual in the course of his work, he would investigate it thoroughly. As he said himself, "Give me facts."

There was always a certain twinkle about his mouth and eyes when he was talking to you, which somehow does not get into a report of his work. His private life revealed quite a different person. His home in later years was in Chelsea and his club the Chelsea Art Club. His friends were mostly artists. He drew quite well himself, and loved dressing up for the Chelsea Art Ball on New Year's Eve.

If he was frustrated by lack of support, he never showed it. His loyalty to his old chief, Sir Almroth

The discoverer of penicillin.

Wright, never wavered. We were never allowed to criticize the Old Man, even when we thought he was being unfair to his colleagues. They had an affection for each other that strengthened them both right to the end of their lives.

The Institute that bore their joint names lasted independently only for as long as they ran it, for, with the coming of the Health Service, such independently supported laboratories and hospitals had to join either a university or the Health Service. Fleming chose to have it go to London University and, when its business interests were wound up, it became a department of the medical school.

When Fleming died, tributes to him poured in. Eloquent obituary notices appeared in newspapers and medical journals throughout the world. "Fleming," wrote the leader writer of the *British Medical Journal*, "had the real naturalist's capacity for observation and the scientific imagination to see the implications of the observed fact ..." There were many simpler expressions of respect, such as that shown by flower-sellers in Barcelona who emptied their baskets in front of a tablet commemorating his visit to their city. Indeed, Fleming would have appreciated such tributes as these more than all the speeches and essays of his colleagues throughout the world, just as of all the monuments erected to his memory he would have most liked the one set up at his birthplace, Lochfield farm in Ayrshire, which bore the simple inscription:

ALEXANDER FLEMING
DISCOVERER OF PENICILLIN
WAS BORN HERE AT LOCHFIELD
ON 6TH AUGUST 1881

Date Chart

1683   Antoni van Leeuwenhoek first sees and describes bacteria.

1835–6   Agostino Bassi shows that the silkworm disease *muscardine* is caused by a tiny fungus.

1866   Louis Pasteur shows that another silkworm disease *pébrine* is also caused by a living organism.

1877   Pasteur proves that anthrax is caused by the bacillus first noticed by Pollender in 1849.

1880   Pasteur succeeds in attenuating, or weakening, an anthrax culture for use in vaccination.

1881   Alexander Fleming born on 6th August.

1884   Elie Metchnikoff shows that white cells in the blood pick up and digest invading germs.

1895   Fleming arrives in London and starts work as an office clerk.

1896   Almroth Wright announces the discovery of his typhoid vaccine.

1897   Fleming goes to the Polytechnic, Regent Street.

1899–1902 The Boer War in South Africa.

1900   Fleming joins the London Scottish Regiment.

1901   Fleming's legacy and scholarship enable him to study medicine at St. Mary's

1902   Wright appointed Professor at St. Mary's.

1906   Fleming joins Wright's department.

1908   Fleming passes his final medical examinations, winning the Gold Medal of the University of London. He also becomes a Fellow of the Royal College of Surgeons.

1909	Paul Ehrlich shows that "606" (salvarsan), one of the first successful modern chemotherapeutic agents, is active against the germs that cause syphilis.
1911	Fleming uses Ehrlich's salvarsan successfully in the treatment of syphilis.
1914	The First World War begins. Fleming serves in France at the 13th General Hospital in Boulogne.
1915	Fleming marries Sarah McElroy on 23rd December.
1918	The war ends. Fleming returns to St. Mary's, where he is made Lecturer.
1920	Fleming appointed Director of the Department of Systematic Bacteriology and Assistant Director of the Inoculation Department.
1922	Fleming discovers lysozyme.
1928	Fleming made Professor at St. Mary's.
1929	Fleming discovers penicillin.
1936	Leonard Colebrook at Queen Charlotte's Hospital announces the successful use of sulphanilamide.
1939	The Second World War begins. Fleming appointed sector pathologist at Harefield.
1940	Howard Florey and Ernst Chain publish the results of their work on penicillin.
1941	First human patient treated with penicillin.
1944	Fleming knighted.
1945	The Second World War ends. Fleming, Florey and Chain win the Nobel Prize for Medicine.
1946	Fleming becomes Principal of the newly renamed Wright-Fleming Institute.
1949	Sarah Fleming dies.
1953	Fleming marries Amalia Voureka on 9th April.
1955	Fleming dies on 11th March.

Glossary

ALLERGY   A reaction to something that has no effect on other people, e.g., rashes from eating particular foods, sneezing from grass pollen, horses or cats, rashes from chemicals.

ANTIBIOTIC   A chemical made by one living creature which destroys others. The penicillin moulds make antibiotics against bacteria.

ANTISEPSIS   The use of simple chemicals to destroy germs.

ASEPSIS   Careful technique to avoid introducing infection.

ATTENUATE   To make a culture of germs harmless without actually killing them.

BACILLUS   A rod-shaped organism. The word is used usually for special groups such as typhoid (*see illustration on p. 25*).

BACTERIUM   A living creature too small to be seen without a microscope. The word is often used loosely to refer to any germ.

BACTERICIDAL   Which kills bacteria; this can be an ordinary chemical or one made by the body.

CHEMOTHERAPY   Treatment by drugs or other chemicals.

COLONY   A group of bacterial cells growing together, usually all coming from the same parent cell.

CONTAMINANT   Any microbe arriving by accident onto a culture.

ENZYME   A chemical made in a living cell which acts on other substances to break them down by digesting them, or to build them up into new substances.

GLOBULIN   Part of the blood fluids responsible for the body's defences.

IMMUNOLOGY   The study of the defences of the body.

LYSOZYME   An enzyme present in body fluids which dissolves many bacteria.

MYCOLOGIST   Someone who studies moulds and fungi.

PATENT   An arrangement to protect a discovery for the benefit of the discoverer.

PATHOLOGY   The study of disease.

PHAGOCYTE   A cell which eats up bacteria.

PHAGOCYTOSIS   The process of eating up bacteria.

STAPHYLOCOCCUS   A spherical bacterium that forms grape-like clusters (*see illustration on p. 64*).

STREPTOCOCCUS   A spherical bacterium that forms chains (*see illustration on p. 64*).

STRAIN   A culture of organisms selected out and kept pure.

SUBCULTURE   The transfer of a small part of a culture to a new container to continue its growth.

SYPHILIS   The most serious venereal disease, caught from an infected person by very close contact.

TETANUS   Lockjaw, a spasm of muscles due to the toxin of an organism, the bacillus of tetanus.

TOXIN   A poisonous substance made by microbes.

TOXOID   A modified toxin which can be used to prevent the disease.

TUBERCULOSIS   A disease often of the lung, caused by a very persistent organism. It is also known as consumption.

VACCINE   A preparation made from cultures of organisms which are safe to inject into people to create immunity.

The words germ, microbe, micro-organism—or "organism" for short—and bacterium are interchangeable.

Further Reading

Almroth Wright. By Leonard Colebrook (Heinemann Medical Books, 1954).

Lysozyme. President's Address (Proceedings of the Royal Society of Medicine, Dec. 1932. Vol. 26. Section of Pathology pp. 1–14).

"On the Antibacterial Action of Cultures of a Penicillin, with Special Reference to their Use in the Isolation of *B. Influenzae.*" (British Journal of Experimental Pathology, 1929. Vol. 10. p. 226).

The Life of Alexander Fleming. By André Maurois (Jonathan Cape, 1959).

The Birth of Penicillin. By R. Hare (George Allen & Unwin, 1970).

Picture Credits

The author and publisher thank all those who have lent, or given permission, for reproduction of the illustrations which appear on the following pages: Birmingham Accident Hospital, 63; Centre D'Optique et D'Electronique, 24; Conway Picture Library, 84; Mrs. Ursula Craddock, 60; Farbwerke Hoechst, 31, 32, 33; Glaxo, 69; Imperial War Museum, 36, 38, 76; Keystone Press Agency, 67; *London Scottish Regimental Gazette,* 12; Mary Evans Picture Library, 29, 34; W. C. Noble, 62–3, 63; Pasteur Institute, 24–5, 25, 26 *top left*; Pfizer Ltd., 72, 74, 75; Radio Times Hulton Picture Library, 40–41, 82, 87, 88–9; Frederick Ridley, 60; R.A.M.C., 18–19, 20; Royal Institution, 27 *bottom*; St. Mary's Hospital, *frontispiece, title page,* 10, 30, 39, 42–3, 47, 49, 51, 55, 58; Sir William Dunn School, 65, 68, 70–1; C. James Webb, 61. The remaining pictures were supplied by the author and by the Wayland Picture Library.

Index

References to pictures whose captions contain information are included.